# Ordinary Magic

## Raine Sillito

BookLeaf Publishing

Presentation by *BookLeaf Publishing*

Web: www.bookleafpub.com

E-mail: info@bookleafpub.com

ISBN: 9789357612661

First edition 2022

# DEDICATION

For Juniper, Hawk and Florence who
continually bring magic into my life

# ACKNOWLEDGEMENT

Thank you to all the powerful women in my life who have shown me the way to be strong, soft and creative.

# PREFACE

When I became a mother, I found myself getting lost in the routine tasks of motherhood - doing laundry, washing dishes, preparing meals and changing diapers. And yet in all the routine, my heart continued to ask deep questions and wonder about the world. When I found myself lost in my own questions or stuck in the daily grind, poetry brought be back to myself. Poetry helped me find space for the wonder in the day-to-day routine of being mother. Letting me capture the magic of making coffee before the early morning rush, the joy in the slow afternoons broken up by laundery and stories with the children. This collection of poems is a window into the ordinary magic of being human, of mothering my children and myself.

# Ordinary Magic

Poetry uses the things around you,
the lemony soup smell drifting
'round the kitchen,
curled cats outside the window -
even those battered lilies
standing on the bookcase

the muddle of blankets
on the rocking chair and
shower water trickling
down the drain -
the smile on a child's face
as they eat toast and jam

Poetry uses the dream
of new running shoes
and the worn socks
drying on the radiator -
the dazed and sleepy child
stumbling down the hall

Poetry uses the blades
of dry grass crunching
under your feet,
rustling wind in the trees -
the rumbling in your stomach that

reminds you, you missed dinner

Poetry makes use of it all,
gathers it up - the entirety of
your human experience
Mixes it together, blending
the magical with the mundane
of this present moment.

# This Moment

This moment holds
a growling stomach
and the faint edge
of a headache -
the wildness of not knowing
settled by the sound of breath

In this moment, holding
the image of a steaming
cup of tea - pen searching
on paper, cool light
filtering through a dirty window
and the buzz of a text unread in

This moment, wild and
uncertain with the memory
of grief and high delight.
Thoughts tumbling along
the rim of my mind - clinging
to the silence of a sleepy house

Thank you impermanence
anything is possible
this constant flux is the only surety
I cling to - because in this moment

of delightful insecurity
everything is possible

# Monday Morning

It's still early, still dark.
I can hear the steam hissing from the kettle
and the usual early morning rumble--
"Have you seen a hairbrush anywhere?"
"Hurry up, I need to brush my teeth!"
Slam, bang the door closes with
a whoosh of cold air.

Then I see the boy and his mom
leaving the next house racing
to make it to school on time,
they stumble in the morning darkness
like they only just woke up
and the boy has a backpack on his shoulder.

They don't say anything, these two.
Just climb into the car and slip away

The sky is starting to bleed with light
and the trees peel out of the dark
and stand against the purple sky

Such beauty that for one moment
the hustle and bustle of a monday
morning can't touch it

then unexpectedly the dog escapes
by way of the swinging front door
and the moment passes
in another early morning scramble.

# Poetry, Found

Today, I decide to search for Poetry
I explore dusty tables, hand knit bags
and crowded closets for
Elusive poetic bits

Poetry hides in the light clicking
of the keyboard, late homework
pressing the keys to a flurry
of activity

It is found in the plaintive sigh
of little fingers struggling
with the teeth of a woolen
zipper.

In the icy shards of a
broken lightbulb on the floor
Poetry leaps upwards and
nicks my fingers

Supper dishes in the sink
Clamor for soap and water
And the bubbles burst, each
expelling a hiccup
of poetry found

I see poetry hiding
everywhere now,
peeking out from behind
the numbers in the clock
the footprints
in the carpet

When loneliness creeps up
I will open my eyes
and find the poetry
hiding everywhere
around me

# Daily Medicine

There is medicine to be found
in the hum of your daily living

the sound of your own heart
beating in your chest

the way cool wind floats
across your cheek on a hot day

the smell of fresh bread
cooling on the kitchen counter

the softness of the
blanket thrown across your legs

the sheer - aliveness -
of each sensation

reminding you, you are here.
and that is enough.

# Today

This questioning spirit
finds awe in the
wonderment of being

there is a small magic in
the smell of lilacs flowering
along the old fence

found again in the steady
sound of rain slapping
against the windows

and in the sleepy baby's
gently rising chest
and rosy cheeks

to be human is to quest.
to ride the waves
of uncertainty
with curiosity and delight

# Just Another Day

Sleepy eyes
in a near dark morning
struggling to focus
on the light seeping
under the door in a wakeful way.

If you collected early
morning thoughts--
the wispy muted ones
that surface when
the first sunlight slips
through the window--
perhaps you'd have enough
to fill a jar, and save them
for dark winter mornings.
letting them warm up
the frosty room,
holding back the cold
with the light of
summer memories.

But its finally the tumbling
of the cats across my feet that pull
me into another day.

# To Do List

To do; recall lost days
  (the faded memories of
  hazy summer sundays)
pay last months rent
return Janie's books
donation to goodwill
  (the things you know you
  never use, but can't ignore)
sew Rose a blue blanket,
or maybe green
call the invisible local
  (to see if he's coming home
  sober)
the car parked on the lawn yesterday
the window in pieces, alas, broken
the bottles in the rhododendrons

To do; remember, don't tread on the
rhododendrons
get the tires rotated
clean the dirt tinted windows
Mow the front lawn--
  (But the lawnmowers broken)
Fix the lawnmower

why does no one ask?
we are solo embers
come see! we exist here

To do; water the backyard plants
pick up the bills
watch the time
  (yeah, there's not much left)
park the car on the drive
answer the ringing phone
keep existing here
  (it's all you can do)

# Our Stories

There is meaning in the peonies
growing along the barn

The hawks soaring silently
over the power lines

Saskatoon branches heavy
with purple, ripe berries

Wild roses blooming in
the ditch by the highway

Heavy gray clouds, almost
bursting with autumn rain

Dandelions clutched in sticky,
sweaty fingers

What stories do you tell yourself
in the evening twilight?

There is immense beauty
to be found in the simplicity
of your very own story.

The fading light around
the dinner table,
the stories before bedtime

the poetry of your own life
rolling around on your tongue
as you move through this day

# Prescription for Happiness

Let go, slow down
be at home with yourself.
Sit in the moment
and draw up happiness
like water from a deep well

To find it you must stand still,
breathe deeply in and out.
walk your way out of conflict
with your stillness and
stay connected to contentment.

Enjoy your grief -
you'll miss it when its gone.

Last week, loneliness chased me
with his strange long face.
No matter what turn I took to
get home, loneliness found me.

And yet, standing in line
at the post office, happiness
struck me, for no reason at all
and left me giddy with delight.

There is no prescription
for happiness - no recipe
to follow.

But if you stay with yourself,
happiness will find you.

Our lives are not linear,
moving onwards like
a highway.
Not linear, no.
We live in pools of movement,
We get lost, then we are found.
The eddies carry us forwards
and sometimes round and round.

So touch honest intimacy -
embrace your wailing
inconsistencies -
there is magic in your own
ordinary life.

# Forgetting is Lonely

we shouldn't forget
that the universe moves
with us.

intangible light
existential trauma notwithstanding -
the stars wheel with us
through this drifting space.

we shouldn't forget time is infinitesimal
a tiny line drifting across
an expanding horizon
a small piece of an even smaller pinprick of
light,
fierce life

we shouldn't forget love is short
and the warmth of a smile a
fleeting delight
but the distractions of being human
make the forgetting much easier

we shouldn't forget the nights between our
separate
hearts are part of this expansive universe,

like dust on the wind it all comes back to us one
day.

we shouldn't forget the rhythm,
the light that emerges in the day to day-
we shouldn't forget that we are born loving
without knowing how or why
or from where -
we love simply from first breath,
from the first anxious struggle into life
into the last moments and the last breaths.

we shouldn't forget the light dance
kisses make across the
distance between us towards no sure arrival -
because forgetting is lonely.

# Divinity

this immovable soul
touched by the immensity
of the inevitable
disappearing of stars
clings-
in this shower of darkness
-to the roots of that tree
inextricably connected
to life

the truth of this one life
held for a moment in
the sound of waves
tapping the shore
and the rustling grass
the spiral shape
of a snails home
and even the sand
between your toes.

it's all that holds us
together--the fragility
of this life held
by the certainty of
not knowing everything

and the wonder of
knowing nothing.
and somewhere in
the sound of birds
in the trees and the hum
of passing traffic
there is inescapable
divinity.

# Ordinary Adventure

if you ask me,
what grand adventures I hope for

if you ask me,
how to change the world

if you ask me,
what kind of mountains
I want to climb

what kind of life i want to live

I would say that we all have
undefinable longings

i would say this never ending normalcy
of dirty dishes and shift work
in the day to day space
that is seemingly endless

keeps me stuck in the ordinary

i would say
i don't know how to change the world
i don't even know how to pay last months

gas bill

i would say,
i feel it--the yearning for adventure
that sits in the bottom of your
lungs and pulls the breath
in and out

i would say

in the just another day space there
are seemingly endless lists of
ordinary to do's

get the oil changed
return the library books
fix the drafty window
put air in the tires
dig up the weeds in the lawn
(but the yellow ones seem so happy)
finish the presentation for Monday's class
don't forget the ringing phone
and the chicken for tomorrow's lunch--

and it just piles and piles on

so if you ask me
if you ask me
how i plan to change the world

i would fumble a bit
avoid the question

i would say
i would say that this house is
too chilled in the winter air
and that i'd really just prefer
a really strong cup of coffee

but i'll take the tea all the same

i would say that this line is
taking too long--do you really
need to get that five cent
discount on hot dogs?

but it wouldn't accelerate the process

i would say that people
who believe in God
are plagued by severe doubts
that never seem to settle

but i don't need to remember the doubt

and i would say

i would say adventure

is the vague desires that
linger on the lashes of the sleeping

but you won't stop asking--
how will I change the world?

so i'll tell you the truth.

The truth is
the electric kettle's not working
 but
dancing barefoot on an icy floor
while the dog sniffs breakfast
is an ordinary sweetness

the truth is
I sit here  and look at all the people here
And wonder at
the miraculous diversity
Here in this one place
Teeming with hopes and dreams
Griefs and losses
And maybe its ok
maybe its ok

If we're not all trying
To change the world
Because  we're changing
The world right now

With every breath
That these lips expel
Because we exist here

The truth is

its not about changing the world
or finding an adventure

its the stop and go
lights the tug and
ebb and flow
of everyday life that
continues to dazzle

It those minutes
When you feel  the pulse
Of your own life pressing against
Your own skin
And the way the grass whispers against your feet
That make you realize this is what  is like to be
alive

The truth is
Adventure  is
is held in the quality of silence
between you and me
After a deep conversation

Because you've taught me that if
there is anything left to
believe in it is the light
left behind in the last star
disappearing as the sun
steals over the horizon

and only these hands remain,
left open, as every other door closes

the truth is
there is something extraordinary
In the intermittent conversations
And the light in your eyes

The kind of possibility that holds the
answer to all the
world's discontent

and the weight
of your smile is one I will
carry out of this moment
to the next

you and I
me and you
orbiting
closer and closer
anchored by

the fragility of this life.

there is movement in this life
that is inexplicably grand

and when light flickers
over the horizon it begins
to blaze a trail of
incredible discovery
that will last well past
any darkness.

# Autumn Rain

Wet air clings to my coat,
Puddles ripple around my feet
As water pours into the gutter grates

Clouds of air puff from mouths
As people hurry into warm homes
and waiting cars.

The bright blue door in the brick
House on the corner looks
distant, as the misty air swirls.

The streets are bare and quiet
the chill in the air signifying
the beginning of work and study.

The tall birch is crying,
droplets falling on my head
as I pass underneath

On this chill september day,
I am alone outdoors
waiting for nothing.

# Motherhood as Meditation

There is only this moment
between movement
when the slow rise and fall
of a childs chest holds
time infinite

and lungs expand
to fill the silence
while the mind darts
through possibility

until finally settling
back into the rhythm
of breath moving
in and out

because this moment
between movement
is rare and delicious
a precious kind of gift

that only those who
have spent hours awake
in smooth blackness of night
milk-stained and weepy

can truly understand.

# When Women Gather

When women gather,
Women bloom like
Spring flowers unfurling
To reach for the sun

When women come together,
Their hearts crack open
And the wild wide energy
Of the stars passes through them

And like sunbreak reaching
Over the horizon they
Shine in the light of
Their shared radiance

And with nothing left
To hold them back
They put down roots and
Continue to blossom

Because when women gather
Women change the world.

They remember they are worthy

They remember, they are magical
Ancient and elemental
They step into their power
Transmuting their pain,
Alchemizing their fear
Clearing the road for
Those who come behind
Pouring life giving water
Into the soil of their souls
So they can rise rooted,
And flourish.

Because when women gather
They bloom.

# Life as if it mattered

Sunlight streams through leaves
dappled summer warmth
laying across my skin

to be human is to
love and be loved.

to feel the discomfort
of a buzzing mosquito
and sit on the grass anyway.

to feel the pain of grief,
skinned knees and
the frustration of
time moving too fast -

and choose to live fully
 anyway.

# Walking Devotion

Walking along the river tonight,
the sun turning the water shades
of blue, orange and pink.

Cotton candy clouds
floating across a
darkening blue sky

By the time we reach
the bridge, long shadows
fall across the pathway
and the street lights
begin to wink on, one by one.

The sheer beauty of
tonights sunset
leaves me breathless
as the children tumble
around my feet,
darting on and off the path,
questions leaping from
their mouths like fireflies
flickering above the water.

Why does the sun set mama,

what makes the lights flicker?

Where do the stars go when
the sun wakes?

These are the moments
I live for - the wonder
in the wandering.

The way the silver
of the moon winks
in the eastern sky,

the relentless curiosity
of unfolding human beings
the task of bringing love
to each moment
in the simple act of
devotion to this one life.

# Star Trail Night

I gazed towards the gentle glow
that was slowly disappearing.
stars appeared apprehensively
from their twilit hiding spots.

The ghostly fog in front of me
was my warm breath sliding
into the darkness as I
shifted from foot to foot.

This was a star-trail night.
The moon no longer visible,
the clouds long since gone,
a stunning visage left behind.

Light against dark. Dark
against the light.
Something stirred inside me
my arms outstretched
to embrace the sky.

# Every Day Magic

Let a tree take root in your heart
expand it wide to let in the newness
found in the delight of seeing
the world through your children's
eyes.

Let fear melt into the sky as
lungs expand to catch your breath,
hope spiralling outwards as
you finally realize the
eternal, undying love that
the universe shares with you
everyday.

From the warmth of the sun
on your face in early mornings
to the fire sky sundown evenings
spent sitting next to the ones
you love

What more can we do with
the interconnected weavings
of our souls?

Allow yourself the

luxury of risk by opening
up like a budding leaf to
the possibility that
the love you want
is no other place.